THE LITTLE BOOK OF CHESS TIPS

PETER FRENCH

THE LITTLE BOOK OF CHESS TIPS

PETER FRENCH

A.
Absolute Press

First published in Great Britain in 2007 by
Absolute Press
Scarborough House, 29 James Street West
Bath BA1 2BT, England
Phone 44 (0) 1225 316013 **Fax** 44 (0) 1225 445836
E-mail info@absolutepress.co.uk
Web www.absolutepress.co.uk

A catalogue record of this book is available from the British Library

ISBN 13: 9781904573685

Printed and bound in Italy by Legoprint

The winner of the game is the player who makes the next-to-last mistake.

Savielly Tartakover

1

As obvious as it may sound,

pay close attention to every move your opponent makes. Why did he make that particular move? Is there an immediate threat that you need to defend against? Can you work out his long-term plan?

2

Remember Emanuel Lasker's advice:

'When you see a good move, wait – look for a better one!'

Try to find the best move you can in every single position.

3

Always have a plan in mind.

What are you trying to achieve in a few moves' time? An attack on the king? The capture of a weak pawn? The break-up of your opponent's queenside pawn formation? The blockading of an an enemy piece? If you just go from move to move, it will not be difficult for your opponent to identify and counter all your threats.

4

Remember

that pieces increase and decrease in

value according to the type of position.

So although a rook and a pawn are roughly equal in value to two knights, the knights will be far more valuable in the middle game while there are still lots of pieces and pawns on the board.

5

Make it a habit to play over every competitive game you play, especially the losing ones.

You will only **avoid repeating mistakes** if you can locate and understand them in the first place.

Analyse your games: look especially for major turning points and take time to understand better your opponent's plans with the benefit of hindsight.

6

Every beginners' book emphasises the need for rapid development of pieces – with good reason.

Time is a vital element in chess. Try to establish all your pieces on the strongest possible squares in the fewest amount of moves, and keep your pawn moves to a minimum, especially in the opening.

7

Never lose sight of the battle for control of the centre. **Control** of the four central squares is an essential element in every game of chess, partly because pieces in the centre have more influence over the board than pieces at the sides, and partly because control **of the centre** enables the player to transfer his pieces from one part of the board to another more quickly.

8

The immediate safety of your king is the single most important factor in any position – **never compromise or neglect** it. Many games are lost by one player launching an attack without making sure that his own king is safe first. Castle as early as you can, and move the three pawns directly in front of **your** castled **king** as little as possible.

9

Know when it's advantageous **to swap pieces.** Generally speaking, the player with the initiative is well advised to keep as many pieces on the board as possible, whereas the player under pressure will usually benefit from equal exchanges of material. However, if one player is actually ahead on material, he will almost always benefit from further exchanges.

10

If by exchanging material you can **weaken your opponent's pawn formation,** that is a very strong reason for doing so. Doubled, isolated or backward pawns are a considerable long-term weakness in any game; do not miss an opportunity for creating such weaknesses in your opponent's structure.

11

Consider

the implications of all your moves for

the endgame.

It may suit your immediate purposes to open a file by giving yourself doubled pawns – but what about when the dust has settled on the middle game and you move into the endgame with equal material? Your doubled pawns may now amount to a losing disadvantage.

12

Concentrate all the time!

If you have a winning position, you still have to win it. Conversely, you can still draw or even win from a losing position if your opponent makes an error – which most opponents do at some point to a greater or lesser extent.

13

If you're **losing in the endgame,** do **set** as many **stalemate traps**

as possible. It's so natural for the winning player to restrict the losing player's moves as much as possible that it is very easy for him to overlook the fact that his opponent is on the verge of running out of moves altogether.

14

When considering the influence of a bishop, rook or queen, whether yours or your opponent's, always follow the line to the edge of the board, no matter what pieces or pawns are in the way. By doing this you will

be much more alert to your own attacking possibilities, and also be readier to defend against future threats, or even to remove them completely.

15

If one of your pieces is pinned or tied, always seek to **relieve the pin/tie as soon as possible.**

The longer your piece is pinned/tied, the more opportunities for game-winning tactics there are for your opponent, and the fewer options there are for you.

16

If your opponent is **moving** a piece **to ‘discover’ a threat from another piece,** you must ensure that you consider every possible move of the moving piece. Occasionally (but rarely) it is possible to allow your opponent a discovery, as none of the possible moves carries a threat.

17

All games are eventually decided by tactics. The player whose pieces are on the most advantageous squares when the tactics begin is usually the winner, even if he didn't foresee the exact nature of the tactics.

18

Pinned, tied, trapped, undefended or insufficiently defended pieces are all **indicators of tactical possibilities. Always be on the lookout** for these elements in both your and your opponent's position.

19

There are **many** reasons to sacrifice material. Gaining time, opening a rank, file or diagonal (especially near the king), obstructing the line of defence between two enemy pieces, decoying an opposing piece (often the king) to a square where it will be vulnerable to a combination, deflecting a piece away from defensive duties – all of these and more are

reasons for making a sacrifice. You need to be aware of all of them to maximise your own winning opportunites, and limit your opponent's.

20

Defend with the weakest available piece

whenever possible. Use pawns to defend pieces as much as you can.

21

The knight is the weakest defensive piece,

because it cannot move at all without giving up its defence, whereas all the other pieces can at least move on the same rank/file/diagonal and still maintain the defence.

22

Any piece that is defending two or more important squares can be said to be overloaded.

Look out for and **exploit overloaded pieces** in your opponent's position as much as possible, at the same time guarding against having them yourself.

23

Don't spend all your practice time learning opening theory

– it's a serious and common mistake. Far too many average players are quite strong in their chosen openings, but fail to understand even quite basic middle game concepts. In any case, a thorough grasp of strategy and tactics is a far greater asset in the opening than mere book knowledge.

24

When you're not sure of the best plan,

improve the position of your worst placed piece.

25

Pawn handling is one of the most important factors in any game. You must strike the correct **balance** between advancing your pawns to create space (and restrict your opponent's), and not making too many **pawn moves,** thereby creating weaknesses in your position that will be exploited later in the game.

26

If your king is under attack,

consider the possibility of simply running away. Sometimes the best defence is to transfer your king to a safer place on the board, rather than trying to defend him where he is.

27

A **mating attack** in the middle game will usually require a minimum of queen and two other pieces.

Never begin an attack **with insufficient material** available.

28

If your king is castled behind unmoved pawns, never forget the possibility of back rank mates. And note that having an entire rook tied to defending your back rank is a seriously limiting factor in your position.

29

Look for possibilities on either side for **the Greek Gift sacrifice.**

This involves the sacrifice of a bishop on h7, bringing the king into the open, and is often followed by Ng5. Factors that strengthen this sacrifice include a bishop on the c1-h6 diagonal, a pawn on e5 (preventing a defending knight from occupying f6), and a rook developed onto e1 that may join the ensuing attack.

30

Another very common sacrifice is **the exchange sac** – giving up a rook for a crucial defending minor piece. Sometimes this sacrifice is tactical and can win immediately, but it is often used to create a position in which the attacker's minor pieces are all active while the defender's are in bad positions with few options. **Look for opportunities** to make this sacrifice.

31

Never begin an **attack unless and until** you have a tangible positional advantage.

32

Do not begin an **attack on the flank unless** you are also strong in the centre.

33

Spend time studying endgames. One good reason for this is that there are frequently opportunities in the middle game (or even the opening) to exchange down into an endgame. The player who understands the endgame better is not only more likely to win when it arrives, but will be much better able to bring about the favourable and potentially winning endgame in the first place.

34

Do not underestimate the power of **the king** as an attacking piece **in the endgame.** Endgames are frequently decided by the simple matter of whose king is the most active, and indeed can end up simply being a race. Do not delay in transferring your king to the part of the board where he can be most influential.

35

In rook v bishop endgames, the crucial principle is that the defending king should try to reach the corner which is the opposite colour of his bishop. This gives the best possibilities of drawing.

In rook v knight endgames, the knight should stay as close to the king as possible.

36

Aim to exchange so that when the endgame is reached it is your opponent, not you, who has a rook pawn. While a single pawn is often a winning endgame advantage, the chances of winning are greatly reduced if the pawn is a rook pawn.

37

If you are **defending with king against king and pawn,** aim to block the pawn before it reaches the seventh rank. This should enable you to draw the game.

38

When defending with a rook against pawns, don't let the pawns reach the sixth rank. Two connected passed pawns on the sixth rank will beat a rook, but the rook should win if the pawns have not yet reached that far.

39

Try to build **batteries on files or diagonals.** A battery is two or three pieces attacking on the same line. A queen and bishop on the same diagonal, or a queen and one or even both rooks on the same file make a force **stronger than the sum of its parts.**

40

To cut down on the amount of opening study you need to do, **consider playing a system** in which your moves are broadly the same whatever your opponent plays, rather than studying lots of individual openings. For example, if you play the King's Indian against d4 and the Pirc against e4, many of the ideas behind your moves will be the same and you will be more familiar with the positions in both openings.

41

Remember that opposite coloured bishops, if they are the only pieces left on the board, will frequently lead to a draw even if one side has a material advantage. **If** you are **winning,** beware of exchanging into **an opposite coloured bishop endgame.**

42

Consider playing your opponent, not the board. Assess as far as you can what type of player your opponent is and aim to frustrate him. If he seems a tight, conservative player, aim for complex, dynamic positions with lots of tactics. If he looks like an aggressive player always looking for tactical opportunities, keep the position as closed and as dull as possible.

43

Never neglect your control of the clock. It is not essential always to have more time than your opponent. It is essential to invest your time wisely, and conserve it for when you really need it.

44

Don't give checks for the sake of it. It is frequently wrong to put your opponent in check, as it can simply have the effect of forcing him to improve the position of his king.

45

Do chess puzzles. This is one of the very best ways of improving your tactical ability. Look for them in newspapers, buy books of them, do them on the internet. Take lots of time over them – and don't cheat.

46

Do buy and **use a good chess computer program,** the best one you can afford. Of course there is no substitute for a real opponent, but sometimes there isn't one available. And you can program your virtual opponent to the level you want – usually slightly better than you is the most beneficial for improving your play.

47

Do not fall into the habit

of playing h3/h6 and/or a3/a6 in the opening in the misguided belief that it always improves your position. A valuable tempo may frequently be gained by these moves when there is a bishop to attack, but otherwise they frequently lead to endgame pawn weaknesses.

48

Don’t forget to look for traps.

If your opponent, whom you know to be a reasonably solid player, appears to have left a pawn *en prise*, be suspicious. Check very carefully before taking any apparently free material against a good player

49

Play your best game all the time. If you're playing a stronger opponent than yourself, treat it as an opportunity to learn. There's no shame in losing to a stronger player - there is in just rolling over because you think you can't possibly win in any case.

50

Remember that chess is a game. Be generous to your opponent when you win, and never, ever be a bad loser. Play to win, play aggressively by all means, but treat your opponent with respect, even if you feel their play is poor, or that they won through a stroke of undeserved luck. If you fail to observe these principles, you will get a bad reputation, something it is very hard to lose once acquired. And your opponents will try even harder to beat you!

Peter French

Peter French is a bookshop owner, musican and avid chess player. He solves newspaper chess puzzles in his lunch hours and competes with computer programs into the small hours of too many mornings to count. Whilst not quite having achieved Grandmaster status as yet, he has been playing and enjoying chess for more than thirty years.

THE LITTLE BOOK OF
BARBECUE
TIPS
ANDREW LANGLEY

THE LITTLE BOOK OF
BEER
TIPS
ANDREW LANGLEY

THE LITTLE BOOK OF
HERB
TIPS
WILLIAM FORTT

THE LITTLE BOOK OF
POKER
TIPS

THE LITTLE BOOK OF
GARDENING
TIPS
WILLIAM FORTT

THE LITTLE BOOK OF
CHEFS'
TIPS
RICHARD MAGGS

THE LITTLE BOOK OF
SPICE
TIPS
ANDREW LANGLEY

THE LITTLE BOOK OF
GOLF
TIPS
PETER FRENCH

THE LITTLE BOOK OF
TIPS
SERIES

THE LITTLE BOOK OF
CHEESE
TIPS
ANDREW LANGLEY

THE LITTLE BOOK OF
WINE
TIPS
ANDREW LANGLEY

THE LITTLE BOOK OF
AGA
TIPS 2
RICHARD MAGGS

THE LITTLE BOOK OF
COFFEE
TIPS
ANDREW LANGLEY

THE LITTLE BOOK OF
TEA
TIPS
ANDREW LANGLEY

THE LITTLE BOOK OF
AGA
TIPS 3
RICHARD MAGGS

THE LITTLE BOOK OF
AGA
TIPS
RICHARD MAGGS

THE LITTLE BOOK OF
CHRISTMAS
AGA
TIPS
RICHARD MAGGS

THE LITTLE BOOK OF
RAYBURN
TIPS
RICHARD MAGGS

THE LITTLE BOOK OF
BRIDGE
TIPS

THE LITTLE BOOK OF
CHESS
TIPS
PETER FRENCH

THE LITTLE BOOK OF
FISHING
TIPS

THE LITTLE BOOK OF
GREEN
WILLIAM FORTT

THE LITTLE BOOK OF
KITTEN
TIPS
ANDREW LANGLEY

MARMITE
PAUL HARTLEY
THE LITTLE BOOK OF
MARMITE
TIPS

THE LITTLE BOOK OF
PUPPY
TIPS
ANDREW LANGLEY

THE LITTLE BOOK OF
WHISKY
TIPS
ANDREW LANGLEY

THE LITTLE BOOK OF
TRAVEL
TIPS
MEGAN DEVENISH

Little Books of Tips from Absolute Press

Tea Tips
Wine Tips
Cheese Tips
Coffee Tips
Herb Tips
Gardening Tips
Barbecue Tips
Chefs' Tips
Spice Tips
Beer Tips
Poker Tips
Golf Tips
Aga Tips
Aga Tips 2
Aga Tips 3
Christmas Aga Tips
Rayburn Tips
Puppy Tips
Kitten Tips
Travel Tips
Fishing Tips
Marmite Tips
Whisky Tips
Green Tips
Bridge Tips
Chess Tips

All titles: £2.99 / 112 pages